TRUMPET HANON

75 EXERCISES TO BUILD ENDURANCE & FLEXIBILITY

BY SCOTT BARNARD

HAL•LEONARD®
CORPORATION

7777 W. BLUEMOUND RD. P.O. BOX 13819
MILWAUKEE, WISCONSIN 53213

PART III • ADVANCED STUDY

PREFACE

"What makes a great trumpet player?" That is a question we have all asked ourselves at some point. It is the ability to excite, move, and captivate the listener. This can be achieved only when you have a solid technical foundation. This book aims to provide you with the tools to reach that goal. Seventy-five carefully designed exercises and melodies will challenge you, while touching on various genres, harmony, and musicality—in fun, interesting, and methodical ways.

The book is divided into three sections: Core Technique, Harmonic Technique, and Advanced Study. Where a "performance" is indicated, I've tried to write a proper piece of music rather than a purely technical exercise, though the performance includes elements of the previous exercise(s). Throughout the book, given tempos are only suggestions.

PART I
CORE TECHNIQUE

1. Staccato/Tenuto
Keep the air supported throughout, especially during the staccato passages.

2. Staccato/Tenuto (performance)

Ensure that the staccato notes have a full tone, similar to the tenuto notes.

3. Accents

Exaggerate the accents.

4. Accents (performance)

This simple exercise becomes quite tricky once you add the accents. Allow the accents to produce their own melodic line. Rest wherever necessary.

Flowing (♩ = 120–150)

5. Slurs

First play this exercise as written, then try it with dotted rhythms.

6. Slurs (performance)

This exercise needs plenty of character and flare to sound playful and fun.

Playfully (circus-like) (♩ = 112–130)

7. Long Notes (i)

Use this "whisper tone" exercise to work on your sound. Try to remove any airiness, so you are left with a pure tone.

8. Long Notes (ii)

This exercise is about controlling your air stream. Make sure the pitch remains constant as you change dynamics. Use a metronome and rest wherever necessary.

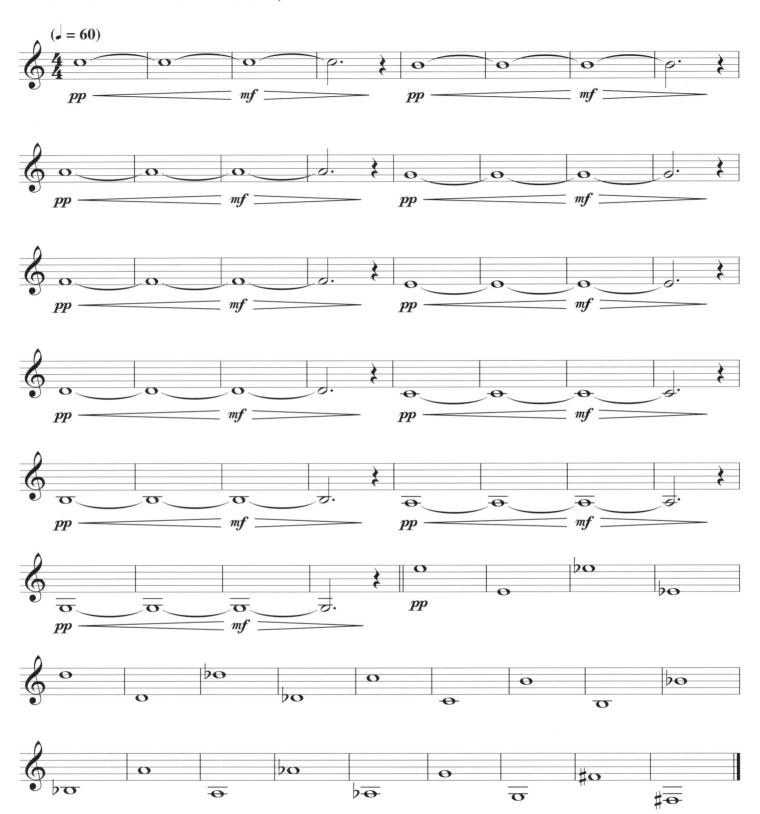

9. Long Notes (iii)

Listen to the quality of your sound. Make sure that there is an even tone throughout the exercise. Use a metronome.

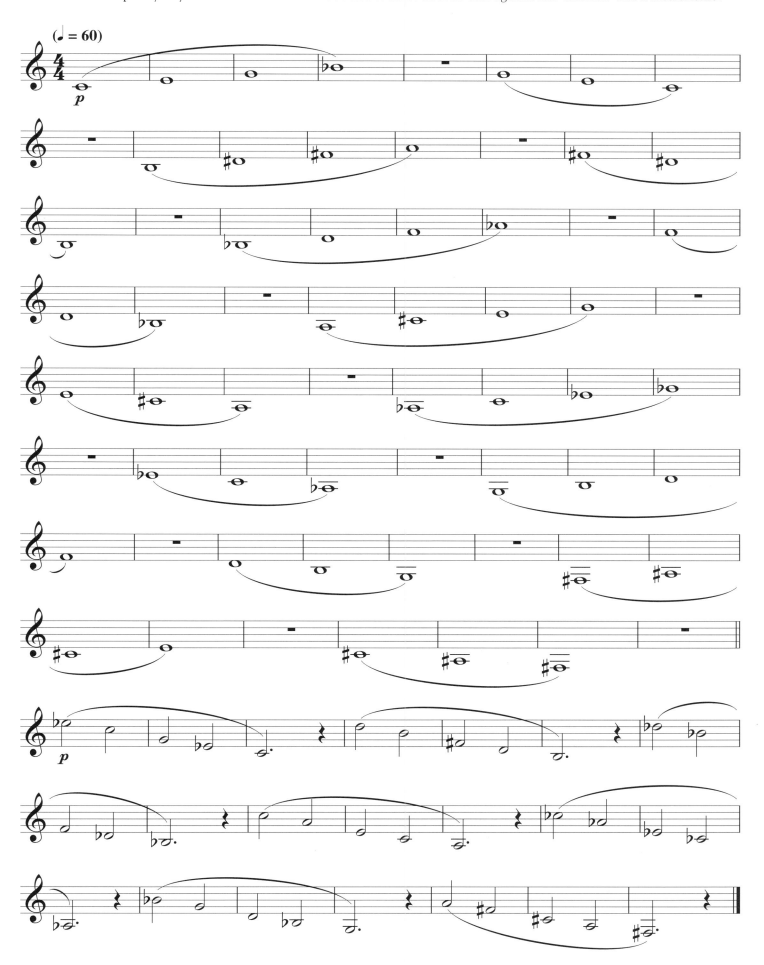

10. Rhythms (performance i)

Make the staccatos really short and punchy. A metronome may come in handy for this one.

11. Rhythms (performance ii)
Use a metronome and internalize the beat.

12. Rhythms (performance iii)

You might find it useful to set the metronome to eighth notes ($\quarternote$ = 210–240).

With a lilt ($\dottedquarternote$ = 70–80)

13. Dynamics (i)

In the first eight bars, exaggerate the dynamics. In the following sections, ensure that the dynamic changes are smooth and graduated.

14. Dynamics (ii)

This is a tricky exercise to master. The dynamic marking in measures 3 and 4 means diminuendo to nothing. Try to make sure that your note is ending in the correct place, rather than fizzling out too early.

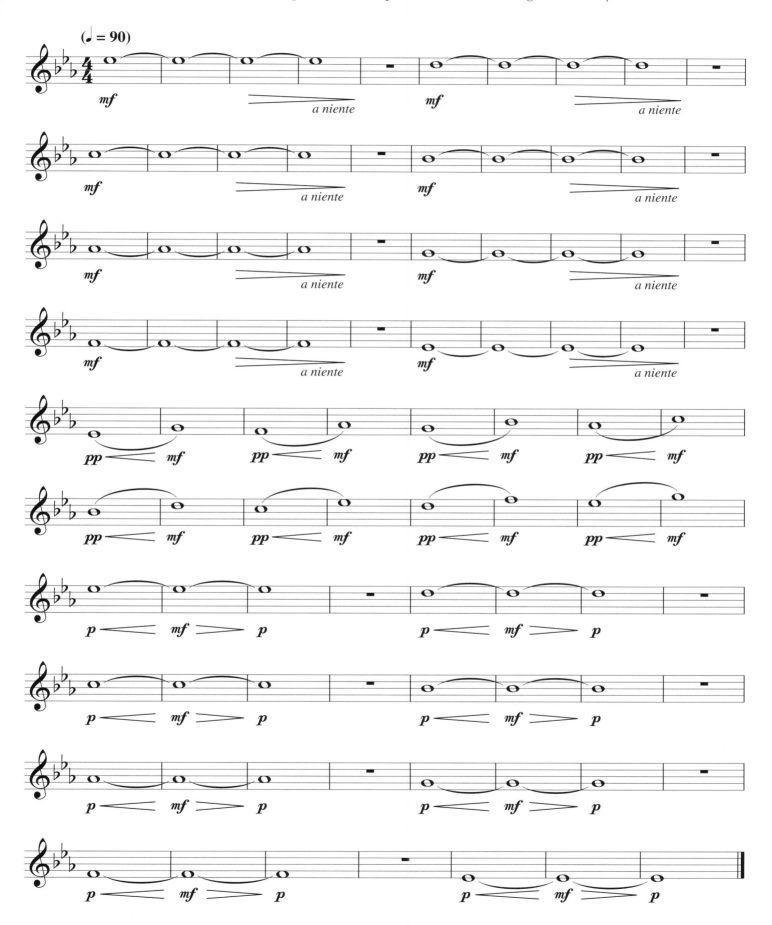

15. Dynamics (performance)

This exercise has some soul/funk elements. Listen to bands like Sam and Dave, James Brown, and Tower of Power to get an idea of the style. The staccatos should be very short. Work on hitting the szforandos really hard, then coming away quickly, followed by a controlled crescendo.

16. Range (i)

Do not overexert yourself with the next few exercises. Go just beyond what you can currently manage.
Over time, this will improve and you will be able to continue further through the exercise. Embouchure strength takes time to build up, so be patient.

The text above the notes is a guide to what your tongue should be doing. Creating these different vowel sounds will encourage your airstream to be at the correct speed for each note. Observe the rests.

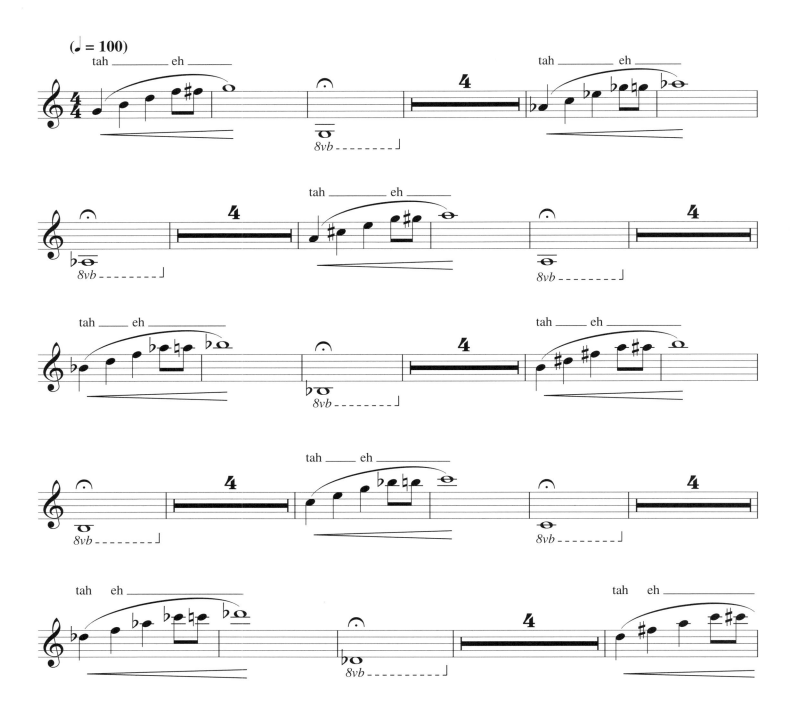

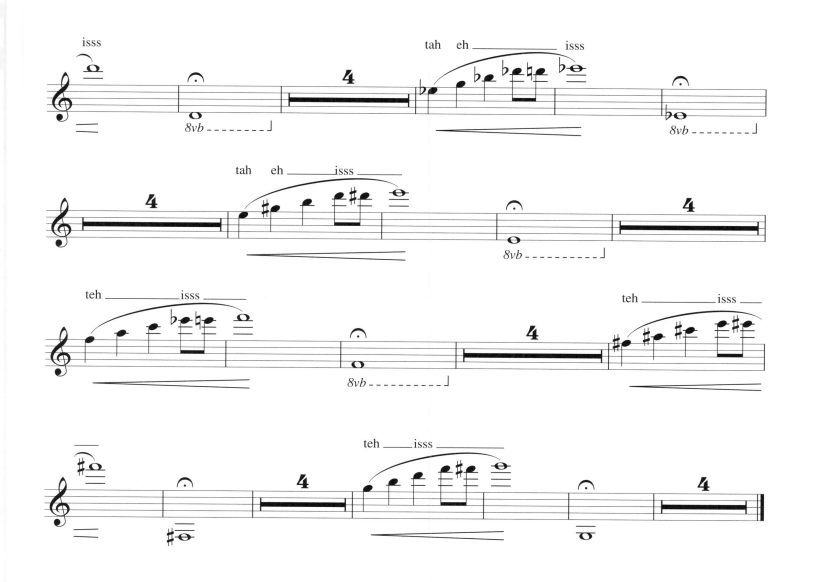

17. Range (ii)

While playing the lower version of each phrase, hear the octave above at the same time. This should help with intonation in the upper register. Again, stop when you are beyond your present range.

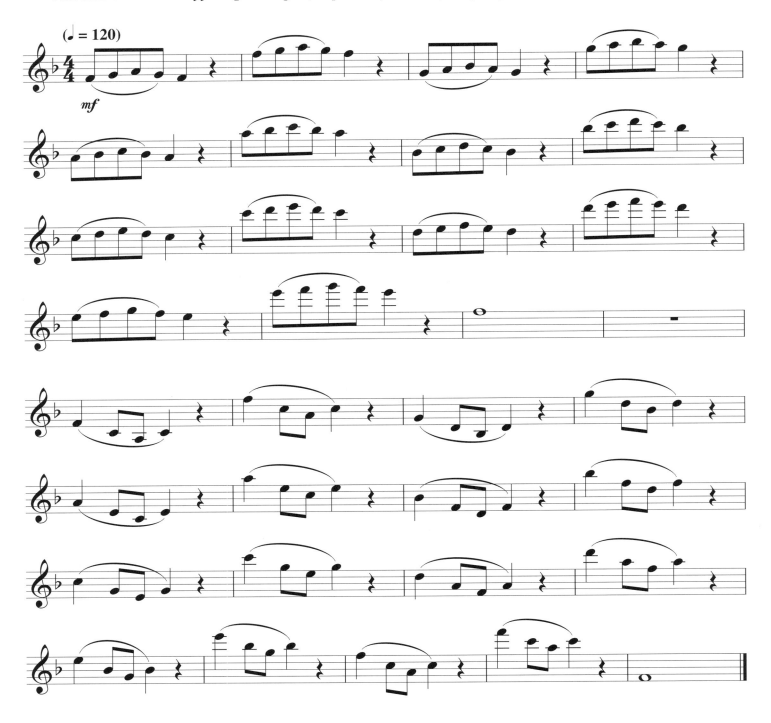

18. Range (iii)

Ensure that you are making a full, open sound across the range of the instrument.

19. Finger flexibility (i)

Practice this exercise slowly at first. Press the valves down firmly.

20. Finger Flexibility (ii)

The rhythmic changes in this exercise will greatly improve your finger dexterity. In general, use this method to work on any difficult passages, as it's a very efficient way to practice. Again, make sure your fingers are pressing the valves down firmly.

21. Finger Flexibility (performance)

Work on getting the musicality to shine through in this one. There's room for a lot of interpretation.

22. Lip Flexibility (i)

Start to work on this one at a slow tempo, ensuring that each note is clean and accurately pitched. Think of each note as a different slot in a pigeon hole rack, like in a mail room. Use a metronome.

23. Lip Flexibility (ii)

Again, work on getting the pitches to sound at exactly the right moment. In the second half of the exercise, make sure that the triplet and 16th notes are precisely rhythmic. Use a metronome.

24. Lip Flexibility (performance)

Here, you will need to master great control to produce a musical performance. Feel free to use as much *rubato* as you like.

25. Single Tonguing

Practice these phrases at a range of tempos. Ensure that each note is sounding perfectly clear before increasing the speed. Extend these exercises by playing them in different keys.

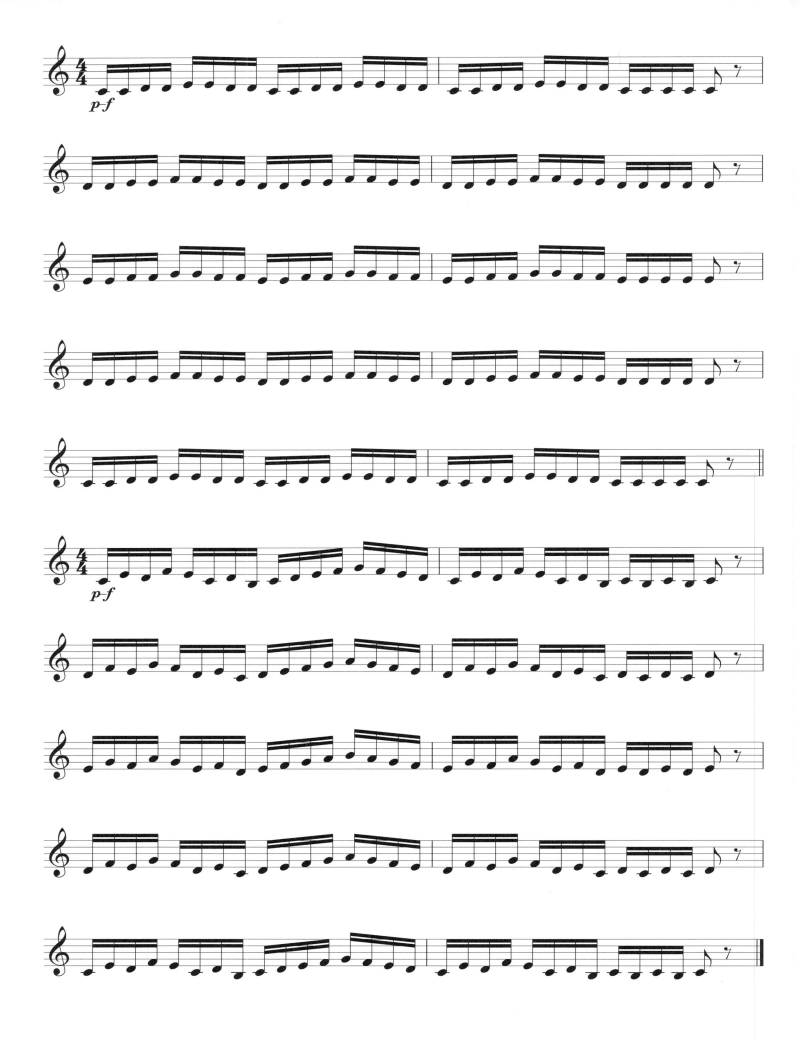

26. Single Tonguing (performance i)

Try to get your production to sound as good in the lower register as it does in the middle register. Use only single tonguing throughout.

27. Single Tonguing (performance ii)

To start, select a tempo at which you can manage the 16th notes comfortably.

28. Double Tonguing

The object of this exercise is to get the "ku" syllable to sound as clean and strong as the "tu" syllable.
Take breaks wherever necessary.

29. Double Tonguing (performance i)

Keep the tonguing nice and light throughout this piece. The accents will help to emphasize the Baroque character. For the mordents above the Gs, use open and third valve.

30. Double Tonguing (performance ii)

Keep the air stream well-supported throughout and observe all the articulations.

Brightly ($\quad$ = 112–128)

31. Triple Tonguing

This exercise calls for the triple tonguing technique and is based on the chord sequence of Johann Pachelbel's *Canon in D Major*. In the last section, accent the single "ku" syllable to ensure that it doesn't get lost.

32. Triple Tonguing (performance i)

In this exercise, the tonguing pattern changes, depending on the rhythm required. Sometimes it may be better to change the triple tonguing order from "tu ku tu" to "tu tu ku" to prevent too many "tu" syllables one after another.

33. Triple Tonguing (performance ii)

In the 3/4 section, the pulse remains the same. Here, you'll need to switch to double tonguing. Take time to spot the patterns throughout this exercise.

PART II
HARMONIC TECHNIQUE

34. Major Scales
These exercises show eight major scale patterns in the key of C. First, play them as written.

Now extend the exercises by:
    a) playing them in other keys
    b) applying different rhythms
    c) using various dynamics
    d) using tongued or slurred phrasing (slur the whole phrase; group in fours or twos, etc.)
    e) placing accents in different places

Here's how you might apply these extensions to pattern #1.

35. Major Arpeggios

Here you have major arpeggios in every key, following the Cycle of Fourths. Each example starts from a different position on the cycle. The last example shows dominant-seventh chord arpeggios.

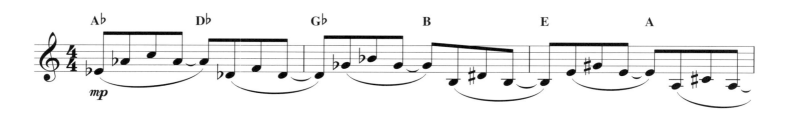

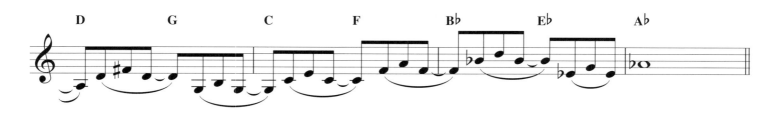

36. Major Scales and Arpeggios (performance)
Take this one at a tempo at which you can manage the triplets.

37. Minor Scales

Here are some exercises covering the three different minor scales. Try them in all the minor keys.

38. Minor Arpeggios

This exercise will help you to quickly recognize all the minor arpeggios and will improve your intonation.
It follows the Cycle of Fifths.

39. Diminished and Half-diminished Sevenths

Diminished seventh chords or arpeggios are based on minor thirds—root, ♭3, ♭5, dim7 (often spelled enharmonically as a major sixth). The chord symbol for a diminished seventh chord can be shown as a circle or as "dim"; it may or may not include a "7": e.g., C°7 or Cdim. Half-diminished seventh chords are similar except the diminished seventh is replaced with a flatted seventh. Half-diminished seventh chords are denoted with a line through the circle, or as a minor seventh chord with a flatted fifth: e.g., C⌀7 or Cm7♭5.

40. Minor Scales, Arpeggios, and Diminished Sevenths (performance)

Make the most of the dynamics and articulations to bring this tune to life.

41. Major Pentatonic Scales

Major pentatonic scales use five degrees taken from the major scale: root, second, third, fifth, and sixth. The following exercises are shown in a variety of keys. Extend them by transposing to all other major keys.

C major pentatonic

D major pentatonic

E major pentatonic

F♯ major pentatonic

42. Minor Pentatonic Scales

Minor pentatonic scales use five degrees taken from the natural minor scale: root, third, fourth, fifth, seventh.
The following exercises are shown in a variety of keys. Extend them by transposing them to all other minor keys.

G minor pentatonic

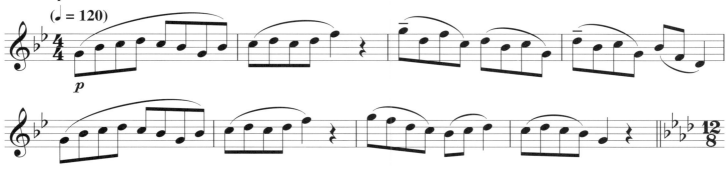

F minor pentatonic

C minor pentatonic

A minor pentatonic

43. Modes

Modes are found in all forms of music, from medieval Gregorian chant to jazz, and from folk to orchestral music. Modes are derived from a major scale; each mode has its starting point on a different degree of the scale. This creates a different order of tones and semitones, so each mode evokes a different character. If we take the scale of C major (all the white notes on a piano) and create modes from it, we arrive at the following:

C Ionian (C-D-E-F-G-A-B)   major scale
D Dorian (D-E-F-G-A-B-C)   minor tonality with raised sixth degree
E Phrygian (E-F-G-A-B-C-D)   minor tonality with lowered second degree
F Lydian (F-G-A-B-C-D-E)   major tonality with raised fourth degree
G Mixolydian (G-A-B-C-D-E-F) major tonality with lowered seventh degree
A Aeolian (A-B-C-D-E-F-G)   natural minor scale
B Locrian (B-C-D-E-F-G-A)   minor tonality with lowered second and fifth degrees

You should be familiar with some of these, such as the Ionian (major scale) and Aeolian (natural minor scale) modes. The Phrygian and Locrian modes are not used extensively, so we will concentrate on the remaining three modes: Dorian, Lydian, and Mixolydian.

This exercise is based on the Dorian mode.

44. Lydian Mode
Remember, the Lydian mode has a major tonality with a raised fourth degree.

45. Mixolydian Mode

The Mixolydian mode has a major tonality with a lowered seventh degree.

G Mixolydian

C Mixolydian

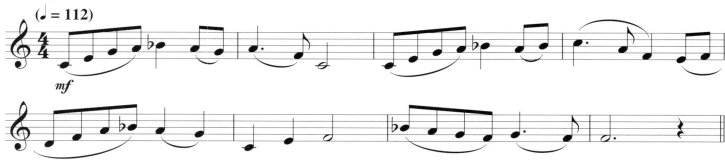

D Mixolydian

A♭ Mixolydian

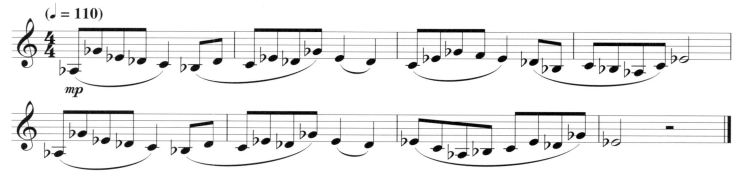

46. Whole-tone Scales

For the sake of simplicity, you can think of there being just two whole-tone scales, one starting on C (C-D-E-F#-G#-A#-C), the other on C# (C#-D#-F-G-A-B-C#). All other whole-tone scales will start from a point within one of these scales.

This exercise begins with a whole-tone scale starting from C. The second part of the exercise looks at the C# version of the whole-tone scale.

47. Whole-tone Scales (performance)

Both versions of the whole-tone scale intersperse this tune.

Confident and quirky (♩ = 72–84)

48. Chromatic Scales

In general, chromatic scales employ sharps when ascending, flats when descending. Always ensure that you push the valves down firmly, especially in the softer sections. To extend this exercise, start it on different pitches, vary different tonguing/slurring options, and experiment with different dynamics.

49. Chromatic Scales (performance)
Think carefully about where you need to breathe, as there are some long phrases.

50. Blues Scale

The blues scale looks like this: root, ♭3, fourth, ♭5, ♮5, and ♭7. The ♭3, ♭5, and ♭7 are known as "blue" notes and give the scale its bluesy quality.

Here it is in every key. A sample bluesy line follows each scale. (Some of the ♭5s have been written enharmonically, for ease of reading.)

51. Blues Sequence (performance)

The blues sequence is 12 bars long, hence the term "12-bar blues." In its basic form it uses one chord per bar and follows this progression:

I–IV–I–I   IV–IV–I–I   V–IV–I–I

There are many variants to this, the most common being to make all the sonorities seventh chords and to replace the last chord with a dominant chord:

I7–IV7–I7–I7   IV7–IV7–I7–I7   V7–IV7–I7–V7

Here is the chord sequence for a blues in G, with the guide tones (thirds and sevenths of the chords) added.

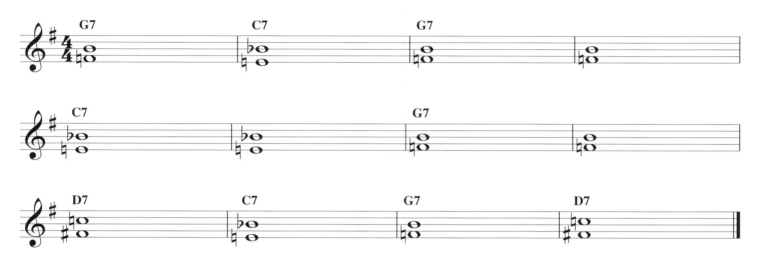

The most common key for a blues is F (G for trumpet). The guitar-based keys of G, A, and E (A, B, and F♯ for trumpet) are also often used. Here is a simple blues based around the guide tones in each of those keys.

Swing (♩ = 148)

Blues in G

52. Minor Blues (performance)

The minor blues sequence is similar to the 12-bar blues, except it's in a minor key. The dominant chord can be either major (V) or minor (v), and the minor pentatonic scale works well for improvising. Here is a sample minor blues solo in various keys. In this example, only the V chord is a seventh chord. The harmony stays on the tonic chord (i) for the first four measures, rather than going to the subdominant chord (iv) in measure 2.

53. ii–V–I Progression

The ii–V–I progression is a harmonic device often used at the end of a chord sequence as a "turnaround." It is also used elsewhere to facilitate a temporary modulation. It's important to be able to spot these progressions, especially when improvising.

In the key of C major, the chords for a ii–V–I progression are Dm–G–C. The ii and V chords are often seventh chords. Here is the ii7–V7–I progression as an arpeggiated line, moving through various keys.

54. ii7-♭II7-I Progression

This exercise shows a slightly jazzier version, where the V7 chord has been replaced with a ♭II7 chord. (This is called a tritone substitution.) This works well because the V7 and ♭II7 chords both contain the same thirds and sevenths, though they are inverted. In C major, this progression would be Dm7–D♭7–C.

55. II7–V7–I Progression

Exercise 55 shows yet another variation. This time, the minor supertonic chord (ii) has been altered to be a major chord, producing II7–V7–I. In C major, this progression would be D7– G7–C.

56. Intervals (i)

The first part of Exercise 56 covers the intervals of a minor sixth to an octave. The rhythm in the second part encourages you to be able to play the intervals quickly and with good intonation. It also serves as a great lip slur exercise. This is a demanding exercise, so rest whenever necessary.

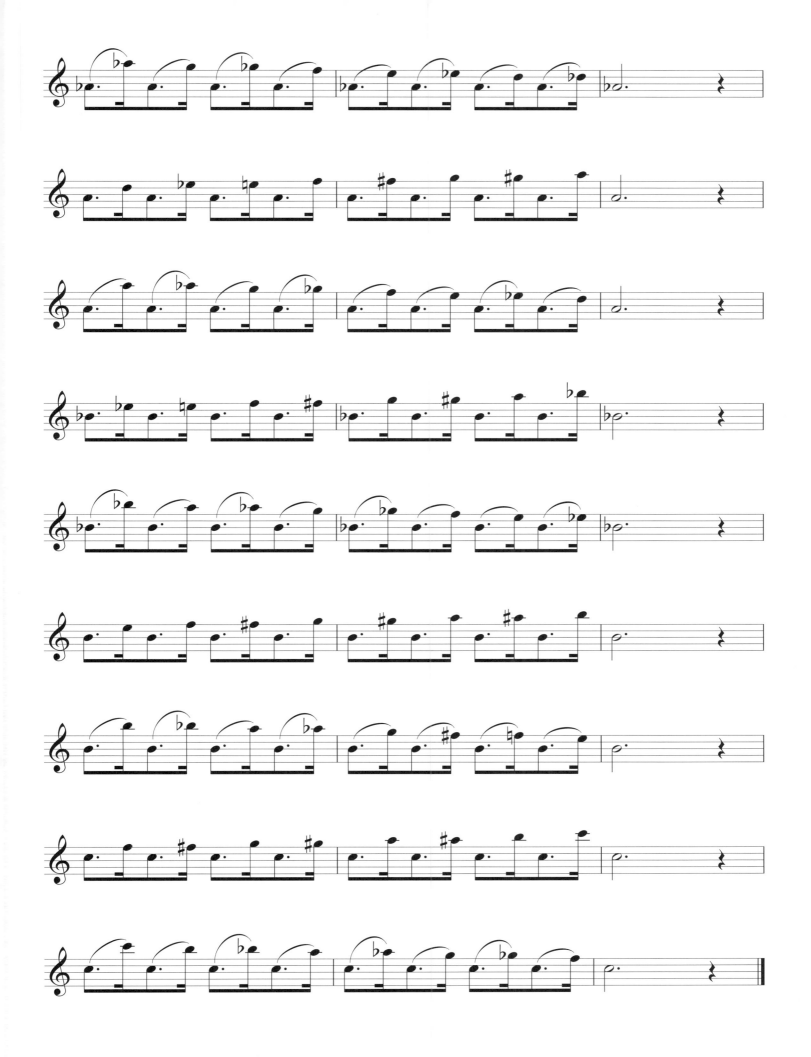

57. Intervals (ii)

This exercise is designed to help you hear intervals that are wider than an octave. Ensure that each note is accurately centered. Avoid clipping any unwanted notes on the way.

58. Intervals (performance)

Here, we explore intervals that are both tongued and slurred. Practice the first section slowly to begin with, to make sure that you have all the correct pitches.

PART III
ADVANCED STUDY

59. 5/4 Time Signature

5/4 is a fairly uncommon time signature, but has cropped up in some memorable tunes, such as Dave Brubeck's "Take Five," Andrew Lloyd Webber's "Everything's Alright" from *Jesus Christ Superstar*, Gustav Holst's "Mars, the Bringer of War" from *The Planets*, and the second movement of Tchaikovsky's Symphony No. 6 (*Pathétique*). In 5/4 time, the pulse is often three beats plus two beats, creating a kind of waltz effect. (In the case of Tchaikovsky's *Pathétique*, however, the pulse tends to alternate between a bar of 3+2 and a bar of 2+3.)

Here's an exercise that includes some of the most common rhythms you'll encounter in 5/4 time.

60. 7/4 Time signature

Even less common than 5/4 is the 7/4 time signature. One notable place that it can be heard is the end of Igor Stravinsky's *Firebird Suite* (originally for trumpet in C). Dotted bar lines indicate the beat division. (Note that the excerpt begins with a bar of 3+2+2 followed by a bar of 2+2+3, but the pattern is not consistent). Imagine a huge timpani note on the rests!

61. Various Time Signatures (performance)

This exercise contains various time signatures. When there are two together, it means that the time signatures alternate, one in each bar (e.g., 6/8 3/4 means 6/8–3/4–6/8–3/4–etc.).

62. Transposition – Trumpet in C and A

Being able to transpose on the trumpet is important, because much orchestral music includes parts that are written for a trumpet other than the B♭ trumpet. Even if you don't play orchestral music, it's still an invaluable skill to work on, because you may be asked to play music not written specifically for the B♭ trumpet.

The easiest transposition is to that of trumpet in C. For trumpet in C, transpose up a step. (This is useful for playing any concert pitch parts.) It may help you to think of playing in a key a step higher, while also thinking about the intervals. Try it out on this example. (You could also go back and try exercise 60, which was originally written for trumpet in C.)

Next, try the same example, but this time for trumpet in A. For trumpet in A, transpose down a half step, again thinking of the new key while concentrating on the intervals.

[Tpt. in C, Tpt. in A]

63. Transposition – Trumpet in D and F

Transposing to trumpet in D can be done by playing up a major third. Think in a new key that is a major third above the original. If it helps, think of each note being on the next line or space up—e.g., an E on the bottom line would become a G# and an F would become an A. Try it out on this exercise.

For a trumpet in F, transpose the key and notes up a perfect fifth. Think of the notes being two lines or spaces higher than the original. Although this works well for tonal music, be aware of accidentals, because these won't be included in your new key signature.

[Tpt. in D, Tpt. in F]

64. Transposition – Trumpet in E♭ and E

Playing a part for trumpet in E♭ or trumpet in E is more challenging. Thinking in a new key may help a bit, but you simply need to know the intervals for these transpositions. For trumpet in E♭, transpose up a perfect fourth; for trumpet in E, transpose up an augmented fourth (or diminished fifth).

The good news with trumpet in E is that you need to know only half of the intervals, because the rest are covered by inverting the intervals: i.e., F = B (B = F), F♯ = C (C = F♯), G = C♯ (C♯ = G), A♭ = D (D = A♭), A = D♯ (D♯ = A), B♭ = E (E = B♭).

Try the following exercise for trumpet in E♭ and trumpet in E.

[Tpt. in E♭, Tpt. in E]

65. Grace Notes – The Appoggiatura (performance)

The **appoggiatura** is shown by a small note (or group of notes) placed before a main note. Generally these should last for half the value of the main note.

The **acciaccatura** (see Exercise 66) is also a small-sized note (or group of notes) placed before a main note. It has a line through the stem, indicating that it should be played as quickly as possible.

In the 17th and 18th centuries, both types of grace notes were played on the beat. In the 19th century, they were played before the beat. Thus, the historical context of a piece often determines how these ornamental notes should be executed.

Here are some exercises using appoggiaturas. Make sure you tongue the start of each group of grace notes.

66. Grace Notes – The Acciaccatura (performance)

Here is an excerpt from the end of "The Ballet of Chicks in Their Shells" from Modest Mussorgsky's *Pictures at an Exhibition*. This was originally scored mainly for woodwinds, so adjust the tempo to fit your current requirements.

67. Mordents

Mordents come in two varieties:

The **upper mordent** is an ornament placed above a note. To play it, you play the main note, the note above, and the main note again as quickly as possible.

An **inverted mordent** is similar to the upper mordent, but it has a vertical line through it, indicating that a lower, instead of upper, note is to be used. Both types can also have an accidental placed above or below, indicating that the note above or below is to be a change from that of the key signature. Here are some for you to try.

68. Turns (performance)

Turns can be quite tricky to to play. A turn should produce the note above the main written note, the main note, the note below, and the main note again. You can also have inverted turns (where the turn starts on the note below the main note) and accidentals above or below (as in the mordents exercise). There are different rules for when a turn is placed between two notes or if placed after a dotted note, so I would recommend consulting a theory book if you're unsure.

This 16-measure exercise is presented twice: first, with turns above, then with a written-out version.

69. Trills (performance)

Sometimes when playing a trill, unwanted pitches can creep in. To avoid this, set your embouchure to buzz at a pitch that is in between the two pitches; e.g., if playing a trill between E and F#, buzz an F♮.

70. Flutter Tongue (performance)

Flutter tonguing is notated with three slashes through a note's stem and usually with some sort of text above: flt.; flz.; flutter. To produce this effect, you need to roll your Rs while playing a note. Tongue the start of a flutter-tongued note as you would any other (unless they are within a slurred passage). Keep the air stream well supported; this is crucial when mastering the opening section of this exercise.

71. Tremolo (performance)

Like the flutter-tongue effect, tremolos have three slashes through the note's stem, but with the addition of some text such as "trem." or "tremolo." This flamenco guitar-like effect is produced by using alternate fingerings; swap between the regular fingering and an alternate one.

Again, keeping the air stream supported is key to this effect. You may find it useful to remove your right-hand thumb from its usual position temporarily, to get a fast shimmer going. Experiment with other finger combinations than those written, to see if another way will work better for you. (A third valve often will work well when playing a tremolo on an open note.)

72. Half-valve Technique (performance)

Using the half-valve technique can add some authenticity to a bluesy solo. This can be carried out in a number of ways, depending on what comes before and after the effect: You can finger the note as normal, while depressing another valve slightly, or go to finger the note but don't depress the valves all the way down. Try out various options on this exercise. On the longer notes, with half valve, release/depress the valve slowly so that you get a variation in timbre.

73. Bends (performance)

To produce a bend, lower your jaw slightly and buzz a slightly flatter pitch. You may find the occasional use of the half valve helps.

74. Glissandos and Falls

To perform a **glissando**, finger the note and, as you are about to play, depress one of the other valves slightly. This will produce a half-valve effect and aid you in moving through the harmonics more easily. If you want an ascending glissando, tighten your embouchure as you go up and change the vowel shape from "ah" to "eh." When you reach the desired note at the top of the glissando, make sure the valve you depressed slightly is back where it should be.

Descending glissandos are similar in that they can employ the slightly depressed valve technique, but the vowel shape will change from "eh" to "ah."

A similar effect to the descending glissando is the **fall**. Unlike the glissando, the fall doesn't usually have a definite ending pitch. Falls can also vary in length, and may have additional text above them such as "long" or "short." You can use the half-valve technique for a fall, but you also can waggle the valves while ripping down through the harmonic series. (This is more commonly done on longer falls.)

75. Glissandos and Falls (performance)

In this exercise, the falls are all fairly short. Be careful not to let them interrupt the pulse.

ABOUT THE AUTHOR

A native of Great Britain, **Scott Barnard** graduated from Trinity College of Music, London, with a performance diploma in classical trumpet. He then went on to be awarded a jazz scholarship on bass guitar.

Over the past 20 years, Scott's playing career has been quite diverse, including engagements such as *Les Misérables*, *Reach Out* (Motown/Temptations national theatre tours), *The Chicago Blues Brothers*, the QE2, function bands, *Opus One* big band, small jazz ensembles, orchestras, and solo recitals.

As a music instructor, Scott has taught many individuals and groups of all ages, in schools and privately, on a variety of instruments. He is the author of *101 Trumpet Tips* (Hal Leonard Corporation; HL00312082).

Scott is also in demand as an arranger, and has provided arrangements for the Raymond Gubbay orchestra, *Don't Forget the Lyrics* (Sky TV), *Sing If You Can* (ITV), and London Orchestrations.

HAL•LEONARD INSTRUMENTAL PLAY-ALONG

Your favorite songs are arranged just for solo instrumentalists with this outstanding series. Each book includes a great full-accompaniment play-along CD so you can sound just like a pro! Check out **www.halleonard.com** to see all the titles available.

Disney Greats

Arabian Nights • Hawaiian Roller Coaster Ride • It's a Small World • Look Through My Eyes • Yo Ho (A Pirate's Life for Me) • and more.

_____00841934 Flute $12.95
_____00841935 Clarinet $12.95
_____00841936 Alto Sax $12.95
_____00841937 Tenor Sax $12.95
_____00841938 Trumpet. $12.95
_____00841939 Horn $12.95
_____00841940 Trombone $12.95
_____00841941 Violin. $12.95
_____00841942 Viola $12.95
_____00841943 Cello $12.95
_____00842078 Oboe $12.95

Glee

And I Am Telling You I'm Not Going • Defying Gravity • Don't Stop Believin' • Keep Holding On • Lean on Me • No Air • Sweet Caroline • True Colors • and more.

_____00842479 Flute $12.99
_____00842480 Clarinet $12.99
_____00842481 Alto Sax $12.99
_____00842482 Tenor Sax $12.99
_____00842483 Trumpet. $12.99
_____00842484 Horn $12.99
_____00842485 Trombone $12.99
_____00842486 Violin. $12.99
_____00842487 Viola $12.99
_____00842488 Cello $12.99

Movie Music

And All That Jazz • Come What May • I Am a Man of Constant Sorrow • I Walk the Line • Seasons of Love • Theme from Spider Man • and more.

_____00842089 Flute $10.95
_____00842090 Clarinet $10.95
_____00842091 Alto Sax $10.95
_____00842092 Tenor Sax $10.95
_____00842093 Trumpet. $10.95
_____00842094 Horn $10.95
_____00842095 Trombone $10.95
_____00842096 Violin. $10.95
_____00842097 Viola $10.95
_____00842098 Cello $10.95

Elvis Presley

All Shook Up • Blue Suede Shoes • Can't Help Falling in Love • Don't Be Cruel • Hound Dog • Jailhouse Rock • Love Me Tender • Return to Sender • and more.

_____00842363 Flute $12.99
_____00842367 Trumpet. $12.99
_____00842368 Horn $12.99
_____00842369 Trombone $12.99
_____00842370 Violin. $12.99
_____00842371 Viola $12.99
_____00842372 Cello $12.99

Sports Rock

Another One Bites the Dust • Centerfold • Crazy Train • Get Down Tonight • Let's Get It Started • Shout • The Way You Move • and more.

_____00842326 Flute $12.99
_____00842327 Clarinet $12.99
_____00842328 Alto Sax $12.99
_____00842329 Tenor Sax $12.99
_____00842330 Trumpet. $12.99
_____00842331 Horn $12.99
_____00842332 Trombone $12.99
_____00842333 Violin. $12.99
_____00842334 Viola $12.99
_____00842335 Cello $12.99

TV Favorites

The Addams Family Theme • The Brady Bunch • Green Acres Theme • Happy Days • Johnny's Theme • Linus and Lucy • NFL on Fox Theme • Theme from the Simpsons • and more.

_____00842079 Flute $10.95
_____00842080 Clarinet $10.95
_____00842081 Alto Sax $10.95
_____00842082 Tenor Sax $10.95
_____00842083 Trumpet. $10.95
_____00842084 Horn $10.95
_____00842085 Trombone $10.95
_____00842086 Violin. $10.95
_____00842087 Viola $10.95
_____00842088 Cello $10.95

FOR MORE INFORMATION, SEE YOUR LOCAL MUSIC DEALER, OR WRITE TO:

HAL•LEONARD® CORPORATION
7777 W. BLUEMOUND RD. P.O. BOX 13819 MILWAUKEE, WI 53213

Twilight

Bella's Lullaby • Decode • Eyes on Fire • Full Moon • Go All the Way (Into the Twilight) • Leave Out All the Rest • Spotlight (Twilight Remix) • Supermassive Black Hole • Tremble for My Beloved.

_____00842406 Flute $12.99
_____00842407 Clarinet $12.99
_____00842408 Alto Sax $12.99
_____00842409 Tenor Sax $12.99
_____00842410 Trumpet. $12.99
_____00842411 Horn $12.99
_____00842412 Trombone $12.99
_____00842413 Violin. $12.99
_____00842414 Viola $12.99
_____00842415 Cello $12.99

Twilight – New Moon

Almost a Kiss • Dreamcatcher • Edward Leaves • I Need You • Memories of Edward • New Moon • Possibility • Roslyn • Satellite Heart • and more.

_____00842458 Flute $12.99
_____00842459 Clarinet $12.99
_____00842460 Alto Sax $12.99
_____00842461 Tenor Sax $12.99
_____00842462 Trumpet. $12.99
_____00842463 Horn $12.99
_____00842464 Trombone $12.99
_____00842465 Violin. $12.99
_____00842466 Viola $12.99
_____00842467 Cello $12.99

Wicked

As Long As You're Mine • Dancing Through Life • Defying Gravity • For Good • I'm Not That Girl • Popular • The Wizard and I • and more.

_____00842236 Book/CD Pack. $11.95
_____00842237 Book/CD Pack. $11.95
_____00842238 Alto Saxophone $11.95
_____00842239 Tenor Saxophone. $11.95
_____00842240 Trumpet. $11.95
_____00842241 Horn $11.95
_____00842242 Trombone $11.95
_____00842243 Violin. $11.95
_____00842244 Viola $11.95
_____00842245 Cello $11.95